TAMI GARRAWAY

Living with Anxieties

Breaking Trough to a Happier Lifestyle

First edition

This book was professionally typeset on Reedsy.
Find out more at reedsy.com

Contents

1

Introduction

For more than ten years, I worked as a manager for Taxes and Sales for furniture, taking care of invoicing and auditing tasks. For more than ten years, more or less the same routine ordered the variables of my life. The order serves me well, helps me relax, and makes the burden of obligations more bearable. It relieves me of that uneasy feeling that I have to be there for my family, give my son everything he needs, and take care of everyone's financial well-being.

For more than ten years, things hadn't changed much—until 2014, when I was told I had anxiety issues.

From that moment, I stopped working. Something unexpected for me, who had historically diligently commuted to the office to perform my duties. But at that moment, I didn't want to go anywhere.

At first, it wasn't easy. My son was young, like eight years old. We slept very little at home, plus my dog was sick. The cocktail of stressful situations was such that I asked to return to the office, even if only for a couple of times a week. I needed that space of peace to regain control of the variables and to better fulfill my obligations.

They agreed, and I alternated work days between home and the office for a while. However, the final decision of my bosses was for everyone to go home and work from home. Which, again, I found challenging…but the context had changed.

My son was older, and the dynamics of my home were different. Sadly, my dog was gone, and working at home became much more viable. Besides, I decided to see the glass half full and think of all the happy moments I would have with my family, being there. I thought about how I would see my son grow up, take his first steps and say his first words.

Back to the life I had left behind, leaving my family to sit in an office for eleven hours to fulfill a job I knew perfectly well did not need me there. My whole life was at home for more than a year, and I built my routine around my family. That was until my job forced me to go back to the office, full time, as before.

Of course, I had to go back. I had no other choice. I had to be responsible for taking care of my source of work, which was the bread on the table for my family. However, something had broken. I had changed. I was not the same person I was a few years ago. The pandemic and the home office brought me closer to my family and my son. To take that away seemed totally torturous, unfair, and irreparable.

I returned to the office with a broken heart, to have a hard time, but with the firm inner certainty that it would be a short time. However, being away from my family made me physically and mentally ill. It led me into situations of pure stress, horrible feelings, and, most of all…anxiety. Anxiety and anguish overcame me.

The anxiety first damaged me mentally. Anxiety first attacked my mood and made me more volatile and irritable. Then it depressed me and made me feel the deep regret of a broken heart. My partner tells me about my son asking for me at home, opening the door expecting to see me, and asking me to play, watch TV or take a nap.

Those feelings of anxiety grew daily, and the mental damage turned into physical harm. To get through the anguish, I turned to eating and smoking. Like never before in my life. In a few months, I gained over 12 pounds and began to feel palpitations and shortness of breath. Sometimes I would get dizzy, and sometimes my legs would feel like they were giving out on me. It's all anxiety. All that burden led to panic and helplessness. Until the day I quit.

I quit when I understood I was getting sick and couldn't take it anymore. I understood that I had to preserve my mental and physical health for myself and my family. And beyond all the challenges that lay ahead, with all that a job change implies, it was necessary. I had to regain control of my life, which up to that moment (and for six long months), my anxiety controlled.

If you are here with me, reading these words, I understand that you are going through the same thing, that you have these feelings of anxiety eating you up inside. Let me tell you that it is totally natural, that it happens to all of us, and that the first big step to controlling our anxiety is to recognize it as such.

We will see in the next chapters what it is, how to combat it, and above all, how to take control of your own life. So that anxiety, which will always be there, is not the protagonist but just another feeling. A feeling as natural as the rest of our hearts. It will be challenging, but if you are determined, you can achieve it without any problem.

2

Chapter 1: I'm Human, I'm Anxious

The History of Human Anxiety

Over millions of years of evolution, anxiety became normal when a person anticipates danger or an unknown situation. It is a natural response of our body to react to an emergency situation. It allows the person to take the measures he/she believes necessary to control the potential harm. However, it has to do with the anticipation of the event, not something that happens at the moment.

As human beings, we imagine dangerous situations in our heads. Something that is going to happen or that we imagine could happen in the future. Anxiety has already come into play at the thought or idea of that situation happening.

It is not wrong to respond with anxiety to things we think might happen. It is not bad to feel it because it is totally natural. The important thing is that stress does not control our life. The important thing is that anxiety and stress do not become chronic, but they could.

A Natural Sentiment

The naturalness of anxiety as a human feeling is sometimes a double-edged sword. Anxiety is so ingrained in our being that we do not pay attention to it. It becomes a normal part of everyday life and undermines our spirit. And it is really difficult to realize it in time.

;Understanding that it is natural and inherent to humans (and many other animals) is fundamental to beginning the long road of anxiety control. We must recognize it as our own to treat it.

Anxiety's Ups and Downs

Fear, negative thoughts, lack of control, and excessive worry are associated with anxiety. Some suffer from extreme anxiety, making it difficult for them to carry out their daily activities normally. Still, in measured doses, anxiety can be beneficial on a personal level and in the workplace.

Like stress, anxiety is also one of the most common ailments of the 21st century. Those who suffer from anxiety are often socially stigmatized as a poorly understood disorder. However, in some aspects, anxiety can be useful as long as it is not extreme and leads to psychological problems.

The state of anxiety presents great advantages in some spheres of life, where the anxious person can use this "evil that afflicts him" to get the best out of himself.

Well-managed anxiety allows the subject to focus, keep his concentration and go for his goals. This feeling is similar to excitement or enthusiasm and can be applied as such in daily life.

Trying to Control It

Controlling anxiety is no simple task, but it is not impossible either. If you really set your mind to it, you can do it. Sometimes alone, accompanied by family and friends, and sometimes by professionals if necessary.

It took me a long time, and that's why I'm helping you achieve different techniques. I used them to achieve it. But the first big milestone we must accomplish to start this path is to know ourselves.

To know our body, to recognize the symptoms of anxiety early, and to decide to act on them.

3

Chapter 2: Let's Talk About Anxiety

How Do I Know if I'm Anxious?

Anxiety is natural and present in all human beings. Therefore, know that you are anxious. It's just the way it is.

Knowing that the next step is to know the symptoms of anxiety disorder. Know the red flags our body and mind will raise when anxiety exceeds healthy limits.

These alerts will also allow us to become aware of how our body, mind, and heart work.

Anxiety Symptoms

Anxiety produces a physical activation accompanied by a series of physiological symptoms, such as accelerated heart rate, sweating, dizziness, and shortness of breath.

At the emotional level, symptoms such as fear and anger, restlessness, discomfort or panic, worry, nervousness, and agitation appear.

At the cognitive level, there may be problems with concentrating, thinking, remembering, and mental confusion.

These symptoms present themselves clearly, almost unmistakably, and are the first major warning sign. Something is going on.

The Anxious Body

If your body physically suffers from anxiety, you will begin to notice the following:

- Nervousness, agitation, or tension.
- The sensation of imminent danger, panic, or catastrophe.
- Increased heart rate.
- Fast breathing.
- Sweating.
- Trembling.
- Feeling of weakness or tiredness.

The Anxious Mind

If you do not yet feel or perceive physical symptoms, you may have the conditions in your mind. Watch for the following psychological signs:

- Not being able to concentrate or think clearly.
- Trouble falling asleep.
- Difficulty controlling worries.
- Need to avoid situations that generate anxiety.

Already knowing the symptoms, and paying particular attention to whether any (or several) of them are present in your body, the next big step we must take to advance on this path of anxiety control is that of self-knowledge.

4

Chapter 3: The Importance of Knowing Yourself

Know Yourself to Know Your Anxieties

My first step in beginning to manage anxiety was knowing myself. Even before I knew the symptoms, I understood that knowing what is wrong with us is essential.

Self-knowledge allowed me to anticipate certain feelings or emotions. And when anxiety was already a fact, knowing myself allowed me to find the focus of the problem. That generated that excessive anxiety.

Once we find the focus of the problem, it will be easier to solve it.

Let's Get Introspective!

To know what is happening, it is necessary to take our mind to the field of introspection. We must practice reflection and properly analyze what happens to us, what we feel, and what generates those feelings.

In the case I mentioned in the book's introduction, I knew that the return to the office was the main focus of all my anguish and anxiety. I quickly understood that I had to do something, that it was an untenable situation. If I did nothing to change the case, the only possible outcome was that I would become physically and mentally ill.

Those moments of excessive anxiety, when I felt short of breath or dizzy, were just the confirmation I needed.

It was introspection that allowed me to focus on the problem, and it was my personal decision to try my best to solve it. It is necessary to be able to analyze ourselves internally and come up with an answer as to what it is that makes us anxious. And, from there, to make an effort to find the solution.

Discover Your Power and Limitations

Knowing oneself not only implies knowing what causes us anxiety, but also knowing our strengths and weaknesses to act upon them.

We must know what we are capable of and where the flame of our power lies. Knowing our virtues makes us better, makes us aware of our potential, and is a useful tool for gaining confidence. By trusting in yourself, you will be able to control your anxiety.

Accept that we cannot control everything and relax. However, we must also know our limitations. This will allow us to reduce the pressure that anxiety generates. Knowing everything we cannot control will enable us to get rid of that backpack.

This way, energy, concentration, and focus will be placed where they belong: in everything in our hands. That is where the objectives are achieved.

From the recognition of our anxieties, our strengths, and our limitations, it will be possible to advance steadily on the idea of reducing our stress.

Through these premises, we will finally be able to take back the control we have of our lives, giving anxiety its rightful place.

And with this in mind, the final step is to convert all our intentions into actions. Take the leap of faith and commit to solving the problem.

5

Chapter 4: Recognizing Your Anxieties

What's Wrong With Me?

Nothing is wrong with you. I mean, we all have anxieties, and at some point in our lives, we will suffer from them. But anxiety is an absolutely natural feeling inherent to all humans, and we all live with it daily.

However, if anxiety becomes chronic, it begins to be considered an emotional disorder, which should be recognized and treated as a disease. Because, in one way or another, these disorders become physical and mental illnesses.

The important thing is not to feel guilty or alone in this anxiety issue because the vast majority of the population suffers from anxiety at some point. Also, as I told you earlier, if you are here with me, it is because you want to take charge of your destiny. You want to take care of not only your mental and physical health, but also yourself and your family.

Where Does My Anxiety Come From?

Anxiety can come from many sources, and its causes are often very personal. Depending on the case, it can be more extreme or milder stress causes. For some people, it has to do mainly with financial worries, perhaps the biggest stress factor in the world.

For others, the focus of anxiety may be because they are going through an illness or perhaps have a sick family member. Anxiety in these cases is always present, and dealing with it (besides the fact itself) is a big challenge.

I suffered a lot of anxiety when my son was born for obvious reasons. First child, my first experience, and a whole unknown world ahead. New worries, new problems, and of course, new solutions. When you have children, anxiety is that fear of the unknown and the pressure of having a human being depending on you.

Whatever the cause, it is essential to know the source to act on it. Thus, we can move towards controlling our anxiety feelings and not affecting our life, our behaviors, and above all, our health.

Time for Action!

The truth is, I can immediately recognize the symptoms of anxiety and how it affects my mind, my body, and my soul. I can also see the cause of my anxiety, understand where it comes from, and even imagine where it will go. But the last big step in reducing anxiety is to take action.

Taking action means not just staying with recognizing the problem, but actively looking for ways to solve it. Get informed, get to know yourself, and take action. By making decisions, changing habits, and incorporating behaviors into our lives, we can get closer to the ultimate goal.

Anxiety will always be there. It is not a feeling that can be "eliminated."

There is no way you will stop feeling it, or it will be part of the past in your life. One way or another, anxiety will be an eternal companion from birth to our last day.

The causes of anxiety are not necessarily bad. However, the idea is that it should be a companion. Let it be the co-pilot of our story and let us take the wheel of that vehicle with strength. As we saw, it is a wonderful feeling if we handle it with care and caution. It is our body unconsciously preparing for something. That which makes us anxious is something positive.

Still, the outcome of it all depends on how we handle that anxiety. It will depend on us to understand anxiety as something natural and human, to recognize that we are not alone and have a problem, and to have the courage to want to solve it.

Taking action comes down to that being courageous.

Following all the steps of the long road to control anxiety increases the chances of achieving it.

Knowing the feeling, knowing it is human and natural, knowing where it comes from and how it affects us, and having enough courage to want to do something about it, are all you need to take the final step. Take action.

Expecting anxiety to go away on its own, leaving no traces or scars, is very naïve. That's not how things work. Or at least, they rarely do. It is through action that life gets better.

I can't claim to be an expert on the subject because no one is. Still, the right attitude and positive mindset are fundamental parts of this process. To want to change, improve as a person, and take care of yourself and your family is where the flame of change is lit.

From there, the energy must be born to take our path forward. Get in front of the mirror, look yourself in the eyes, and assume all that you deserve. Assume that you want to be happy. Assume that for this, the anxiety has to be controlled. And with that feeling of power, go out to the playing field to win the game.

You have the chance to win. Everything indicates that you do.

It only depends on you.

6

Chapter 5: The Fine Art of Controlling Your Anxiety

Time to Change Your Life

Now is the time. Now is when we take control of our life, destiny, and everything we want for our existence.

We want to live calmly, happily, and healthily. We want to be good for our families and grow as human beings. And for all this, it is key to control anxiety.

Taking action literally means changing your life. Take charge of what touches you. Own it.

In my case, the anguish and anxiety I experienced during those six months when I returned to the office first transformed into food, tobacco, and stress. My natural response to anxiety went that way, and the cost I was paying was huge.

Channeling my anxiety this way was costing me my mind, body, and life. My affections, family, and body were affected by every minute I spent inside that building. I knew the answer. I knew the way forward, but it was not easy.

It takes work to take action. It's not easy to cheer up. Giving a 180° turn to your life, routine, and work structure requires a lot of effort, sacrifice, and, as we have already said, courage.

I told you, it all comes down to that. And the courage to change, in this aspect of anxiety control, has to do with incorporating behaviors and exercises that help to relax. The mentality is there, and the knowledge and the will to take action are already there. It remains to be seen what to do to reduce anxiety. And if he couldn't "reduce" it, at least use all that anxious energy for good.

We will see below different techniques to control our feelings, especially when we feel overwhelmed. First, it will be a conscious job; you must be attentive and watchful of moments of anxiety to act accordingly.

After a while, when you have incorporated the necessary behaviors to live with anxiety healthily, you will see that it will be more organic. Naturally, your mind will recognize, reduce, control, and appropriately channel moments of anxiety.

That step (that the action becomes unconscious) will confirm that we are on the right track.

Practical Exercises to Control Anxiety

It is necessary to act when anxiety attacks us at that exact moment (not a minute before, not a minute after). It is essential to prevent feelings of anxiety from escalating because, in that case, we could lose the advantage.

Think of it as a battle between you and anxiety, and treat the surprise factor as something to eliminate. Anxiety can't surprise you. It shouldn't. When anxiety strikes (and it will), you must be one step ahead, anticipating everything.

We have to anticipate the level of anxiety, its symptoms, its cause, and its consequences. When I started getting short of breath in the office, I automatically noticed it and acted accordingly. Likewise, when I felt overwhelmed by my surroundings, I needed to leave a room and get some air. Or breathe gently to slow my heart and breathing rates.

Here are practical exercises to use whenever or wherever anxiety strikes to help you refocus.

Deep Breathing

One of the most effective ways to reduce stress in the body is through practicing deep breathing. By taking a deep breath, it acts like a signal to your brain to calm down and relax. And when the brain identifies this message, those factors that occur when you're stressed, such as increased heart rate, rapid breathing, and high blood pressure, decrease accordingly.

Breathing is directly related to physiological activation and anxiety reactions. We tend to hyperventilate by taking short and too fast breaths or, on the contrary, taking two deep breaths and large breaths.

In both cases, we get more oxygen than we need. And it doesn't feel good.

To reduce alert levels in certain situations, learning and integrating forms of controlled breathing into daily life is very useful.

If we pay attention to our breathing, we will also promote relaxation and functionality of the muscles.

We will take air through the nose, slowly and deeply. As we do this, take a moment to feel our chest expanding.We count to three, filling our lungs well with air and holding the air for 3 seconds. We feel how the air is loosening our muscles and joints.

Finally, we will slowly release the air through the mouth, counting to three again. You can do it steadily, pushing the air out of your body, or you can do it in small bursts. The important thing is to be slow.

Repeat this process two or three times to reduce your heart and breathing rates during anxiety. Remember that it is only a moment, and then it passes.

Progressive Muscle Relaxation (PMR)

Edmund Jacobson developed this relaxation method after he realized how closely anxiety and muscle tension were related. He understood that reducing one reduces the other. And it is especially useful since we can use it at times when we notice more anxiety or nervousness.

In the same way, regardless of having previously experienced complicated or stressful situations, it is advisable to reserve a few minutes every day to practice this technique and master it to take advantage of all its benefits.

The technique's purpose is to cause mental tranquility by suppressing all muscle tension in the body, learning to progressively relax all body parts.

Sit or lie down in a comfortable place and follow the next steps:

- Start with your head down, tensing as many muscles as possible for five seconds. Your forehead, cheeks, and whole face should feel that muscular tension.
- Then begin to slowly relax her. Think about the feeling of total relaxation for at least ten seconds. Feel how the muscles lose that tension and relax.
- Next, you will do the same with the eyes. Close them by squeezing the eyelids hard. Feel that force and that pressure. Then slowly begin to relax the area as much as you can until they are ajar.
- You will continue with your nose and mouth same dynamic. Tension is first for five seconds, then ten seconds for absolute muscle relaxation.

- You continue with your neck and chest, then your arms and legs. Go tensing each of your muscles and then releasing that tension. Press your hands hard, and strain your biceps and triceps. Then repeat with the other arm.
- With the legs, we do the same process.
- To tighten your back, lean forward until you feel pressure in the middle. Tense all the muscles you can. If you bring your elbows back, it will be better. After that, return to your starting position and relax the muscles.

Meditation

Meditation is an old technique used by our ancestors for thousands of years. The original intent of meditation was to help understand the sacred and mystical forces in life. In recent days, meditation is more known as a method for relaxing the soul and a stress reducer.

Meditation will help you learn to stay centered and maintain inner peace. It will benefit your emotional well-being and general health. You can also use it to chill and deal with stress by focusing on something calming you down.

The benefits of meditation continue even after the session ends. Practicing regular meditation can help you go through the day more calmly and manage the symptoms of certain medical conditions.

There are different types of meditation, but the main steps are as follows:

- To get the most out of meditation, get to your most comfortable position, but try to maintain a good posture.
- If you are a beginner, practicing meditation will be easier in a quiet place with minimal distractions.
- Keeping track of your attention is one of the most important

elements when we talk about meditation. Focus your attention on your breathing, your heartbeat and your body.

- You can focus on things like an image, an object, or even your breath to free your mind from outside distractions. You can also use mantras, short phrases you repeat over and over again to stay focused.
- This technique involves deep breathing to slow your heart rate and reduce the use of the muscles in your shoulders, neck, and upper chest.
- Eventually, you will meditate anywhere. You will have the necessary practice to apply this technique at any time, place, or circumstance that warrants it.
- Keep a receptive, open, and positive attitude.

When Should You See a Professional?

Anxiety may be only a small part of a more complex problem. In these cases, it is always recommended to ask for therapeutic help to get to the core of the conflicts that generate them.

Knowing whether it becomes a chronic and recurring feeling or just something temporary is essential. You should treat anxiety with a specialized doctor if it is a constant.

We can control anxiety, but up to a point. Acute cases of anxiety represent such an extreme situation that hardly a breathing exercise or meditation calms you down. The person suffering from these attacks can literally feel like they are dying. It should not be taken lightly, and you need the guidance of a professional.

If your anxiety episodes are at this level, see your trusted doctor and start treatment. Remember that it is important to know how to ask for help and to let yourself be helped if necessary. Remember that we are human beings, infallible, and have limitations.

When we hit the wall of our limitations and cannot solve the problem alone, we must allow others to help us. May we be receptive and optimistic with help and go for it.

7

Conclusion

After quitting my job and eliminating that focus of ill-gotten anxiety, I felt much better. That day I returned home, hugged my son, and repeated to myself the importance of the step I had taken. Convinced it was the right thing to do. Convinced it was the job or my mental and physical health.

When health is at stake, the choices are few. I would say only two. Leave things as they are, or take charge of the situation. Many people opt for the first option, sometimes out of fear or unwillingness. They sweep the anxiety under the rug, and the results are catastrophic.

However, the fact that you have made it this far means quite the opposite. It implies you understand the issue's importance and the potential seriousness of mismanaged anxiety, and you want to do something about it.

The idea of this book is primarily to raise awareness of the issue and to provide the reader with the tools necessary to make progress. This is achieved through understanding and action.

Understanding has to do with incorporating the premise that anxiety is a natural feeling of every human. As such, it cannot be eliminated. It is not erased, nor can it be annulled. It has been with us forever and will be there daily.

Trying to eliminate anxiety would be nonsense. What is necessary is to control it. To do this, first, we have to recognize it as such to take possession of it. We must know when it is present, its source and causes, and try to understand where it comes from and where it is going. As we said before, to anticipate the damage.

With all this information gathered, the next step is to take action. Modify our behaviors, incorporating the necessary exercises to reduce, control, and apply for good all that anxiety into our daily lives. It is a lot of energy that, otherwise, is totally wasted.

Turning intention into action is the final step. The most important. It is useless to know our anxieties if we do nothing with them. That quota of courage is necessary.

And that courage, that necessary bravery, does not only have to do with doing the exercises but with a structural mentality for your life. We must have enough courage to assume that if anxiety is winning us over, we need a substantial change in our actions.

Maybe it's work, a relationship, or friendships. It may be the practice of a sport and the pressure it generates. It can come from many places, but of one thing, you must be sure...something must change.

Have full confidence in your abilities and power, and need to improve. Become strong there, and the road will be a little easier. You will slowly see your life, health, mood, and state of mind improve.

And you will feel that wonderful feeling of a goal accomplished, self-improvement, and a healthy and balanced mind.

8

References

5 exercises for anxiety. (2022, January 24). Www.medicalnewstoday.com. https://www.medicalnewstoday.com/articles/anxiety-exercises#how-they-help

33 Self-Awareness Activities for Adults and Students. (2017, September 21). Develop Good Habits. https://www.developgoodhabits.com/self-awareness-activities/

American Psychological Association. (2022). Anxiety. *American Psychological Association*. https://www.apa.org/topics/anxiety

Anxiety Exercises: Mindfulness, PMR & Breathing Exercises for Anxiety Relief. (n.d.). Healthblog.uofmhealth.org. https://healthblog.uofmhealth.org/wellness-prevention/3-easy-exercises-for-anxiety-relief-you-can-use-anywhere

Facco, E., & Zanette, G. (2017). The Odyssey of Dental Anxiety: From Prehistory to the Present. A Narrative Review. *Frontiers in Psychology, 8*. https://doi.org/10.3389/fpsyg.2017.01155

Holland, K. (2018, September 19). *What Is Anxiety?* Healthline. https://www.healthline.com/health/anxiety

How to Identify the Real Cause of Your Anxiety. (2021, September 14). Psych Central. https://psychcentral.com/anxiety/getting-to-the-r

oot-of-your-anxiety

Intention-Action Gap. (n.d.). The Decision Lab. https://thedecisionlab.com/reference-guide/psychology/intention-action-gap

Martin, E. I., Ressler, K. J., Binder, E., & Nemeroff, C. B. (2009). The Neurobiology of Anxiety Disorders: Brain Imaging, Genetics, and Psychoneuroendocrinology. *Psychiatric Clinics of North America, 32*(3), 549–575. https://doi.org/10.1016/j.psc.2009.05.004

Mayo Clinic. (2018, May 4). *Anxiety disorders - symptoms and causes*. Mayo Clinic; Mayo Foundation for Medical Education and Research. https://www.mayoclinic.org/diseases-conditions/anxiety/symptoms-causes/syc-20350961

Raypole, C. (2019, March 15). *Physical Symptoms of Anxiety: How Does It Feel?* Healthline; Healthline Media. https://www.healthline.com/health/physical-symptoms-of-anxiety

Self-knowledge: The basis of everything! | *Central Test*. (n.d.). Www.centraltest.com. Retrieved November 22, 2022, from https://www.centraltest.com/blog/self-knowledge-basis-everything

Talking With Your Doctor About Anxiety. (2019, August 29). Healthgrades. https://www.healthgrades.com/right-care/anxiety-disorders/talking-with-your-doctor-about-anxiety

Understanding Anxiety: The Complete Beginner's Guide. (2017, August 25). Nick Wignall. https://nickwignall.com/understanding-anxiety/

What Is Self-Knowledge in Psychology? 8 Examples & Theories. (2021, July 22). PositivePsychology.com. https://positivepsychology.com/self-knowledge/

When Should You See a Doctor for Anxiety? | *HealthyPlace*. (2017). Healthyplace.com. https://www.healthyplace.com/blogs/anxiety-schmanxiety/2017/10/when-to-see-your-doctor-about-your-anxiety-symptoms

Why Stress and Anxiety Aren't Always Bad. (n.d.). *Https://Www.apa.org*.

https://www.apa.org/news/press/releases/2019/08/stress-anxiety

(n.d.). Https://Goop.com/Wellness/Health/How-To-Calm-An-Anxious-Mind/.

www.ingramcontent.com/pod-product-compliance
Lightning Source LLC
LaVergne TN
LVHW020539160826
845677LV00015B/4144

* 9 7 9 8 3 6 7 6 3 4 7 0 9 *